CHENNAI LATTÉ

A Madras Brew

Ranjitha Ashok

Biswajit Balasubramanian

EastWest Books (Madras) Pvt. Ltd
• Chennai • Bangalore • Hyderabad • New Delhi

EastWest Books (Madras) Pvt. Ltd
571, Poonamalle High Road, Aminjikarai, Chennai - 600 029.
3-5-1108, Maruti Complex, II Floor, Narayanaguda, Hyderabad - 500 029.
53/2, Bull Temple Road, Basavangudi, Bangalore - 560 019.
A-10, Lower Ground Floor, Lajpat Nagar III, New Delhi - 110 024.

Text: Ranjitha Ashok
Cartoons: Biswajit Balasubramanian

First published in the columns of *Madras Musings*

ISBN: 81-88661-31-7

Price Rs. 170/-

Cover concept:
Shalini Biswajit & Lakshmi Srinath

Book design & Production:
J. Menon, www.grantha.com

Printed at :
Sri Venkatesa Printing House,
Chennai 600 026 E.mail: saicure@vsnl.com

Published by
EastWest Books (Madras) Pvt. Ltd
571, P.H. Road, Aminjikarai, Chennai - 600 029.
E.mail: ewb@vsnl.com

Contents

Foreword

I FIRST MET Ranjitha in 1979, when she became an Ashok, in fact, a member of the TTK family. T T Krishnamachari and my father had long been friends, but I got to know the family only from 1968 when I took charge of TTK's printing and publishing unit. When I first met Ranjitha, somewhere along the way in the conversation it transpired that she had been a journalist. That's when I should have persuaded her to get involved with the editorial department of TT MAPS and make life easier for me, but, instead, we meandered into talking about journalism, which she was not thinking of getting into again, at least not then. Whereupon she gave up writing for babies and a children's boutique.

It was in the 1990s that the muse began to inspire her again. I began to read her in *Eves Touch,* the only women's magazine in the South, which I helped by dotting the i's, crossing the t's and minding the p's and q's. I had to do none of that whenever Ranjitha's copy arrived. In fact, I'd flip through the pile to see if there was anything from her, and, if there was, grab it to look at it first. For I was sure it would give me enough laughs to not only sustain me through the rest of the pile but also through the day.

Those pieces Ranjitha did for *Eves Touch* were hilarious. Their razor-sharp wit, caustic at times, resigned at others, and what-to-do occasionally, might have seemed a breath of fresh air to a grouchy editor like me who had by then come to the conclusion that no one had a sense of humour in this country, at least not enough to write amusingly, but it would have made the day for hundreds of mothers bringing up families in Madras and who'd gone through all Ranjitha wrote about without seeing the funny side of things. 'Bringing up Father' had always appealed to me from the time I was young; Ranjitha's 'Bringing up a Family' struck the same chord. My only regret is that, now that her brood has almost flown, she's stopped writing more in the same vein. But she could at least have made a book of it all. Which was advice she didn't heed. But there's still time...

There are many young parents who'd find nothing has changed...not even the need to look at the amusing side of life!

Be that as it may, as the Ashoks grew up and Ranjitha had less to say about them, she wanted to write something different. That was about the time a few readers of *Madras Musings* had written to me saying that the one thing the fortnightly lacked was what all Indian newspapers and journals were short of, a good piece of humorous writing. Would she like to try her hand at amusing, but meaningful, comment, every fortnight, on Madras that is Chennai and maybe someone in authority would see beneath the humour that there were things that needed to be done to make the city a better place and life in it more comfortable? "I've never done anything like it," hummed and hawed Ranjitha, backing away from the thought. But in time to make its appearance in *Madras Musings* on January 16, 2002, there arrived her first piece for *A-musings*.

Supplementing Ranjitha's writing and making *A-musings* still more telling has been the contribution of Biswajit Balasubramanian, the teaming coming about quite serendipitously. One of the first exhibitions at the Forum Art Gallery, run by Biswajit's wife Shalini, was a look at Madras that is Chennai by well-known artist A V Ilango. The way Ilango had handled the chaos that seems an integral part of life in Madras made me ask him whether he'd like to do a regular cartoon for *Musings*. "Wait. I'll bring him here, someone who will suit you to a T," he said. And in moments he was back with Biswajit in tow – and promising me that he was not pulling my leg, that Biswajit could not only caricature, had a good line, but also a sense of humour. When in a few moments I discovered that Biswajit knew Ranjitha, I suggested they work it out between themselves. And as April 2005 dawns, not only is *A-musings* still going strong, with Ranjitha's words teaming with Biswajit's cartoons, but the combination has had enough readers demanding that their work be brought out as a book. And so we have *A-musings* today. I look forward to readers enjoying the best of their work over the last three years.

Whether their comment, trenchant, wry, or just life's-like-that, has made a difference to life in the city, I don't know. I rather think it unlikely, for who in authority anywhere pays heed to newspaper comment or suggestions? But *A-musings* has undoubtedly given pleasure to hundreds of readers. And if there are people like Ranjitha and Biswajit who can make a few smile or chuckle, surely that's enough in a city where both are at a premium.

Chennai
April, 2005

S. Muthiah

WITH MANY THANKS

THE CARTOONS AND articles in this book are based on the columns '*A-Musings,*' and have been previously published in *Madras Musings*. The bi-weekly columns began on 16th January, 2002.

We would like to thank Mr. S Muthiah, Editor, *Madras Musings*, and the members of *Chennai Heritage* for giving us an opportunity to work with them over the years, and for being a source of encouragement regarding this compilation.

Ranjitha Ashok
Biswajit Balasubramanian

ice cream
Biswajit
2005

"Oru Vaa Kapi" or mocha-mint-cinnamon-coffee-latte,
whatever – caffeine rocks everyone's world

A BEAKER OF THE WARM SOUTH

A CUP OF COFFEE.

Good old quintessential southern coffee, with its accompanying images - davara-tumbler, a newspaper, a couple of easy-chairs, a home bustling with morning routine…..

Enough to put any South-Indian-in-exile in a maudlin mood of gooey sentimentality, creating an uncontrollable desire to go around singing 'Thraadishun" in full operatic throttle, until restrained by all right minded citizens with a ear for music.

Doesn't matter. The warbling Southie would have had to stop short just before hitting a high note anyway, simply because coffee has done an about-turn, gone all cool and contemporary on us, and is now being wooed by people noticeably lacking in grey hair.

Now this is a shock, particularly for those of us who grew up in the days when Zeenat signaled 'peace' and the height of cool was defined by a certain soft drink.

Have you seen the number of places that have sprung up, dedicated to the ol' cuppa?

You should have....that's where your children hang out these days.

These shrines to the coffee bean, with their very client-specific ambience, have transformed the home-brew completely. Some of these 'transformations' are so delicious, they are almost decadent.

"It's only coffee." you scoff, proving thereby that you belong to a particularly low variety of *ignoramus homo sapia,* complete with large feet and red ears, who still believe that 'Kapi' is what parents and grandparents drink.

The times, they are 'a changin'.

Time to wake up and smell the ....

(Er...no. That's too obvious, isn't it?) ▮

These younger generation vaathiars prefer cold café latte to South Indian filter coffee!

A growing, spreading wave of rubbish threatens to engulf the city while different species of citizens prove that one living being's...er...rubbish is another's ...umm...feast.

WHAT RUBBISH

FOR SOME TIME NOW, the media has been issuing a dire warning.

"Chennai's garbage too much for 2 dumps", they intone. (Well, eau de Chennai certainly confirms that little news item). This prompted certain well-meaning, industrious folks to set up state-of-the-art garbage bins all over the city. Swanky looking trucks, manned by uniformed staff (awe-inspiring things, uniforms) began to drive around importantly, picking up bins from strategic locations.

Chennai's garbage collection went all contemporary.

Except –

Someone forgot to tell our four-legged friends.

These guys sensed an alien presence in their domain, and rose as one to combat the threat.

The two chief species involved are (naming no names) of the canine and the bovine persuasion, while the feline, with all the suave aplomb its race is so renowned for, reaps advantages without doing any of the dirty work.

The cows, bulls, buffaloes, and our street dogs and cats were perplexed at first at these apparently impenetrable bins. Then, with an intelligence that far outreaches anything a poor human can ever lay claim to, they got it. The cry "Eureka" resounded in strictly non-human circles.

It is all so simple – and effective. They merely get the bulkier of their mates to ram each dust-bin ....(or let's be New-Age – receptacle for aromatically-challenged, rejected flotsam-jetsam)..... ram them repeatedly, keeping up the action with a determination one can only point to with pride, until the poor bin tips over with a defeated sigh. Our friends then feast long and well, inviting friends over, fetching one another from neighbouring streets, sharing and sharing alike.

It's very clear.

You can go as high-tech as you like.

But you can't beat Native Street-Smarts.....Indian Style. ▌

Those days of scouting for food are over... now that a state-of-the-art company collects it for us!

When the gentle touch of ministering angels is applied with just a bit more vigour than one would wish, it could herald the end of civilisation as we know it.

THE HEALING TOUCH

A LOCAL NEWSPAPER carried this horror story which succeeded in raising fresh bogeys in the minds of already sorely-tried Chennai-ites.

Apparently, a reporter, belonging to that paper, went to the ophthalmic unit of a certain hospital right here in the city to merely meet a doctor, when an enthusiastic, but slightly misguided Matron, mistaking him for a patient, squirted dilating liquid into the reporter's eyes.

You applaud the lady's firm, unswerving devotion to duty, although, as a result of a difficult working day, she appears to have started seeing patients everywhere.

But you have to wonder. Assuming that no red-blooded non-patient would have meekly submitted to the attack, didn't she hear the reporter's loud, unmistakable protests? Anyone who has ever undertaken the awful task of applying eye-drops in someone else's eyes knows how difficult it is. You find yourself battling someone who suddenly sees you not so much as a near-and-dear as much as a murderous adversary. Panic sets in. Arms flail violently at you. The head pulls away. Eyes remain stubbornly shut, in spite of repeated entreaties to "keep your eyes open and don't move."

Even threats like "I swear, if you don't stop this nonsense, I'll make you drink the damn eye-drops," don't work.

The process is particularly challenging with children.

So how did the Matron succeed?

Well, it could have been worse.

The reporter might have been on his way to see someone in the vital-organ-transplant section.

What next? ID cards to distinguish visitors from patients, or colour-coded corridors?

"Follow the green line to merely see people; the yellow if you're the one with the problem. And hey, no cheating."

Who'd have thought that well-intentioned visits to hospitals to meet friends and family would be so fraught with danger? ▮

So what if you are a journalist? You will have to have your pupils dilated even to interview the doctor!

Chennai's roads are mute testimony to a favourite adage of the powers-that-be: 'Never let a sleeping, clean, well-laid out road lie.'

HAVE SPADE, WILL DIG

PSST!

Did you know that there is a beautiful avenue, with broad sidewalks and lovely old trees in '——Nagar'?

Make sure you don't tell anyone. Because if you do, the Digging Squad will descend on it like a dark cloud of retribution and begin its fell work.

What is it about the sight of a straight, neat road, with no pot-holes and no unexpected ups and downs that brings out the worst in our maintenance people? They react with such prompt severity that within hours the road looks like it has been in a fight of truly gigantic proportions with a particularly malevolent adversary, and now has no hope of recovery.

Those Chennai-ites who walk, leap from crag to peak like graceful mountain goats while others check for physical injuries at the end of each sortie.

Do you sometimes get a feeling that departments within the powers-that-be complexes never seem to speak to one another?

I have a list of new roads that have been laid in Chennai last week. Can I ask the various departments to draw up their "digging" schedules?

One bunch arrives, digs, lays pipes, then disappears. Then another bunch appears weeks later, digs *at the same spot,* lays wires and cables, disappears. Weeks later, yet another team appears, rips it all up to put down something else, and vanishes. And get this: No one ever fills up the holes.

Wouldn't it be easier for all concerned if these guys sat down friendly-like and talked it over, deciding to do their digging and their installing at more or less the same time?

Shhh.

Word is out on the street: A short stretch of road in '—puram' is smooth and clean.

Remember –

You did NOT hear it here first. ▮

The few weeks of decent weather granted to Chennai in December-January are like a gift of yore from a certain Mediterranean area; they come bearing their own dark forces within – to whit: mosquitoes.

WHAT'S THE BUZZ?

"NOW THAT SUMMER'S HERE, the mosquitoes will disappear", someone, (with an incurable obsession for silver-linings, apparently) gushed the other day.

Well, I hate to burst anybody's bubble, but I can tell you someone forgot to tell our winged, disease-spreading, scratchy-bite creating friends that they are expected to head for the hills in summer.

The city is under a moving, flowing, buzzing curtain of tiny, but deadly, little insects.

The look of the season is 'red bumps and spots tastefully scattered over all exposed areas.'

And conversations are invariably punctuated by short, sharp reports that sound like slaps or gun-shots.

This can be rather disconcerting. There you are, breezing along, conversing amiably on all things non-controversial, when suddenly your fellow-conversee leaps in the air like he's been pierced by a needle, then slaps himself in the face or arm, causing you to do a bit of leaping yourself, mostly backwards, biting your tongue in the process. Well,

You know the new mosquito repellent formula we worked on? It has some minor side effects!

yes, you realise he wasn't going to attack you, but you never know, in these turbulent times. It pays to be on guard, after all.

Everyone has 'the best possible solution' to tackle this problem – herbal, chemical, aromatic - whatever.

I think the mosquitoes are smarter. They listen to our theories, laugh themselves sick, and then proceed to get us, deadlier than ever.

Can you hear that buzz? ▌

When the mere act of slipping into something comfortable after a refreshing bath turns into a grim clash of wills between you and a rebellious garment which clings limpet-like to damp skin, you know Chennai's summer has arrived.

THE HEAT IS ON

HAVE YOU NOTICED how many songs there are about the sun, summer, and how the livin' is easy during tropical heat waves?

The Chennai-ite is in no mood to listen, though.

Dear Sol has always been in fine form over our fair city, and any attempt to extol his virtues might lead to unpleasantness and mob violence.

Every year, Chennai wonders: Was summer this bad, or this prolonged, last year?

The weather stalks you from the moment you waken. You cannot stay still because you are scared you might just congeal and melt and all that will remain as mute evidence of your existence is a small, damp spot on the ground. You cannot sit anywhere because every form of seating known to man, floor included, is burning hot. Lean tiredly against a passing wall, and you'll straighten up in a hurry as the smooth surfaces sear you.

Friendly, easy-to-slip-on clothes turn into violent foes that bunch up into bands around your neck and try to choke you.

Summer? Hot?… no, it's not so bad,
at least not in my house!

The gentlest soul is apt to snap, the doll-iest baby turns hostile, and the fluffiest puppy turns into a T-rex…and who can blame them?

Many years ago, I overheard a comment made by a much-put-upon citizen, who was trying unsuccessfully to mop up a streaming forehead.

"The heat is very hot", gasped this worthy.

Indeed it is…and then some. ▮

Given the average parent's penchant for the "When-I-was-your-age..." speech, it is a blessing that one's children cannot indulge in a spot of time travel, and see how mope-y their parents were as students when returning to school.

CLASS 2-B

JUNE BLUES

THE FIRST WEEK of June.

Chennai goes through a strange Pied-Piper-strikes-again metamorphosis as more and more children disappear through the better part of the day. The commonly beheld expression on most young faces falls distinctly into the 'impending-doom' category.

You can't blame the kids for feeling depressed.

It's tough going back to school after a gap of nearly eight weeks, with doubts and fears a mere adult will never understand.

Will your class contain the same faces? Will you sit next to the same people?

Will your best friend still be the same? Or will you find a horrid changeling instead, who lets you down thoroughly by growing taller, suddenly sporting straight teeth or hair, and talking about bungee-jumping, while all you have to show for your holidays is one sweaty, boring picnic, and a couple of movies?

Physically, I'm in school allright, but mentally, I'm still in Goa!

What happens if groups change, leaving you alone at lunch time? Will your class draw a young, cheerful class teacher, or get stuck with Old Nightmare-in-Chalk, the Scourge of the Staff-Room, instead?

Is your new school-bag just a little too obviously new?

What if you are the only one in class who still hasn't seen the most recent Harry Potter movie?

And all the clueless adults in your life can do is babble: "Oh come on, think what fun you'll have in your new class!"

Yeah, right.

Oh well, there's always end of term. ▮

Among the many beliefs and passions that unfortunately lead to schisms amongst people, few can rival this one - the passion of the Sports-Fan pitted against the exasperation of a member of the 'Sports-Leave-Me-Cold' species.

GOAL FEVER

SAY WHAT YOU want about the advantages of a shrinking world, exclaim all you can over the wonders of global connectivity, especially via TV - there's no denying that there are some stranger-than-usual fall-outs as a result, especially in the field of Sports.

Consider this: Various groups of brightly-clad, enthusiastic – and no doubt very talented - young people kick a ball around a large, open area in a far-away country. Result: one young gentleman goes on a rampage in a totally unconnected distant land - inadvertently, he claims, thanks to a misunderstanding over the TV remote.

And 800,000 toilets flush within a time span of 15 minutes in Yokahama. One assumes that's during a commercial break.

Remarkable.

Chennai, I'm sure, has its own tales to tell.

The citizens are clearly divided – Those who Watch Football, and Those Who Don't.

For the former, life is One Big Party. The latter group, however, consists of morose grumblers, who have been trying for days to have conversations about mundane, but unfortunately essential, everyday topics with the former group, who, while genuinely trying to pay attention, have developed a disconcerting habit of suddenly flying out of their chairs with rousing cries. Or falling back with death-rattle groans. This startles the conversation-initiators into losing their tempers, and sharp words inevitably follow.

The air is thick with jargon - "Red card", "Throw-in", "Header". And "Free-Kick", "Corner-Kick", "Scissor-Kick", "Bicycle-Kick".

One word of warning though.

Do not impart too much information about kicks to Non-Watchers, who might be tempted to come up with a few innovations of their own.

Two worlds – one TV.

Where's a referee when you need one? ▮

This is the last warning... and the next time you miss your target, I will pull out the red card!

Life in Chennai has its share of irony, one of the most prominent examples being the manner in which this city, perched on the shores of a huge body of water, yearns and thirsts for the old H_2O.

PIPE DREAMS

IMAGINE THIS.

Someone goofs up in Cosmic Traffic-Control, thus enabling a former inmate of the Indus Valley Civilisation to glance through the First Chapter in a contemporary history book.

Is he impressed by our cleverness in figuring out their civilisation? Or does he rush back to his particular Era-sharers, laughing himself sick, saying: "You won't believe what they refer to as the 'Great Bath'?"

Interesting concept?

Then consider this.

2000 years from now, someone digs up the ruins of an ancient civilisation, whose people were once known as the Chen-nai-ites.

Of the many things that puzzle them, the most mysterious are those large cylindrical pipe-like things that run for miles, buried along what were obviously once pathways.

Were they dwelling places, they wonder?

Can't be, because there is evidence of a fairly advanced form of architecture.

Hiding places? Or for commercial use, perhaps?

No, neither makes sense. Besides, they seem so untouched, so empty and dry.

Transport?

Unlikely.

Slowly, sadly, the team of archeologists walks away, beaten, acknowledging that this particular civilisation was too smart for them, and would keep its secrets for ever.

Oh well....can't blame them.

How could they guess that the pipes were meant for good old water?

Water - that never came.

Maybe we should leave a note for the future. ▮

Heads, we use these pipes for low-cost housing, tails as kennels for street dogs!

If the powers-that-be wanted us to be a pink and white race, one assumes they'd have factored the colour-scheme into the basic design.

MIRROR, MIRROR

THE CITY HAS BEEN suffering from a rash of hoardings for a while now.

The resultant sense of irritation is worsened by the fact that so many of them advertise fairness creams, tempting even the most gentle of citizens to seriously consider going on a rampage.

What is with this constant obsession with fair skin?

You are actually being sold the idea that this is the one quality which will become your passport to everything – from fun evenings with a visibly upwardly mobile crowd and special treatment in hotels, shopping malls and theaters, to a higher intelligence quotient (go figure!), better jobs, more meaningful, long-lasting relationships – you name it. Life becomes available on your terms....and it is all thanks to the Cream that promises to make you several shades lighter.

As for the claims that are made.

"Fair skin in 4 days", boasts one.

"Ha, we'll do it in 2 days," scoffs another.

Our new fairness treatment is very simple and effective… one coat of putty and three coats of white paint!

A third laughs derisively, and drawls: "Overnight, my friend. That's all we need."

All of which immediately leads to a concentrated rush of prospective buyers to the counters, waving their money, and dreaming their dreams.

You have to wonder – how can anyone buy into these tales?

The guys who spin those yarns however know exactly what they are doing.

They too have heard of that old saying:

"There's one born every minute." ▮

Since the hazards of finding parking seem to provide endless fodder for conversation at social gatherings here in Chennai, one might assume that the city has found its rightful place on that list of 'Great Cities of the World'.

WATCH THAT SPACE

IN TODAY'S Chennai, the fate of any proposed outing hangs upon One Single Factor:

The answer to the question: *"Is it easy to find parking?"*

If the answer is "Yes", go ahead, get dressed up, and take the city by storm.

If the answer is "No", chances are that you will stay home, gazing glumly at the TV, or pretending to read a good book.

Seasoned citizens willing to brave chaotic traffic and nightmarish roads blench at the thought of finding parking for their vehicles.

Even the importance of one's presence at social occasions pales besides the worry over parking.

"Getting married....and at that particular chathram?" you tell your friend, "Well, I'm happy for you, but I cannot cordially grace the occasion. Where would I leave my car?"

Families with wailing, hungry kids raising hell in the back seat, drive briskly by certain hotels. They'd rather bear with the noise than face the torture of trying to find a

Please be patient, sir, our valet has gone to get your car from our own car park at Tambaram!

space to park. And have you seen people trying to quickly slip their vehicles into a parking space even as the earlier, more trusting, and so obviously more gullible, arrival is slowly reversing into the spot?

Talk about being viciously competitive.

Everyday, new vehicles hit the road, but nobody knows where to park them.

Sorry, Chennai...you have no choice.

You'd better learn to walk again. ▮

This is sari-ous, or rather, serious business.
(*Sorry – we are aware that was a bit much!*)

THE WHOLE SIX YARDS

BY THE TIME you read this, the last sweet will have been eaten, those crackers that went un-cooperatively *phtt* tossed away, and spirited arguments of the "Why-should-I-come-with-you-to-visit-old-Aunt-Nasty-Tongue?" variety with one's offspring resolved.

All fun times inevitably carry specific under-currents of tension, but the winner of this season's 'Most Harrowing Experience' title has to be – *sari shopping*.

Have you seen what happens to Chennai in the weeks preceding Deepavali?

"Unbridled frenzy" doesn't even come close.

For days, ravaging hordes scour shops, running here for a discount, there for 'new arrivals', frantically attempting to be in fifteen different places at the same time – all for that elusive Sari that will define this year's festival for them.

The quest involves physical endurance, patience, competitive spirit and grim doggedness. Also willingness to suspend inhibitions temporarily and use elbows and handbags as lethal weapons whenever required. Reaching

No, I'm not riot police! I'm your wife and I'm ready to go to that sari sale!

counters is practically impossible, involving clambering over heads, waving and calling out demands to worn-out salespersons, who become wispy, elusive (sometimes sharp-tongued!) beings whose eyes are hard to catch.

As for the billing process - it takes so long, you begin to wonder if you'll ever see your loved ones again, and even indulge in a wistful 'I-wonder-if-they'll-miss-me' fantasy.

All for what?

The Big Day arrives; you step out in your brand new acquisition – only to hear that the one shop you decided to skip had the best selection and bargains of the season. ■

And the ironies that so highlight the fabric of life in Chennai continue, when a constant prayer for water is answered with a mighty deluge that seems in no hurry to stop, causing some amount of disruption, despair, and dampness.

PATCH OF BLUE

CHENNAI - AND WATER. A topic for endless discussion, speculation, complaint….and hope.

Every now and then, the sky darkens; clouds gather, and citizens get cricks in their necks from all that sky-watching.

This is a situation that can go any which way, because the cosmos has its share of comedians who sometimes get carried away.

They need to be told: Look, we need water, and we do ask for rain. But what we mean is the gentle variety that droppeth upon the place beneath, not an aggressive, in-your-face deluge that would make Noah feel at home.

Of course, our city then does what it does best in an emergency – come apart quite spectacularly, particularly as roads turn into waterways, leading to pale jokes about needing boats in place of those vehicles more commonly seen on city streets.

At times, much-enduring Chennai-ites are further harassed by the cosmic comic crew.

Like the time the day dawned to newspapers declaring: "The cyclone is coming", leading to alarm, dread – and rejoicing among our school-going citizens. Except the sky was suspiciously clear, getting brighter and blue-er by the minute. TV news channels were appealed to. "The cyclone will strike", they reiterated. Citizens glanced at the papers, looked at the screens, and ran out to gaze at the sky, perplexed and confused. Those who had journeys to make, things to do or events to conduct, were particularly harassed by the prospect of difficult decision-making looming ahead.

Telephones began to jangle.

"Is there school?"

"Yes."; "No"; "Can't say".

"Maybe it will rain in the afternoon", said some young hopefuls, watching the clearing sky with dismay.

But it didn't.

And while that was a relief to one and all, one couldn't help wondering – Was that a chuckle, wafting on the now-suddenly balmy breeze? ▮

How many times have I told you not to take the weather forecast in the newspaper seriously?

A myriad variety of vadais, dosais, and what-have-you. And sometimes, inadvertently, a delicate designer-food portion of members of the insect family.

EVENING SNACKS

CHENNAI IS NOW officially a fitness-conscious city, with earnest citizens walking, gym-ing, and dieting.

But those Chennai walkers who use the slightly more wooded open areas for their evening perambulations face unexpected dangers, especially during certain seasons.

Apropos of this, a rule has been established - while they can keep their eyes open, they must keep their mouths shut, because members of the insect community make a habit of flying in on suicide missions. And, while one respects all species, one draws the line at swallowing something with hair, wings and legs as a snack, especially when one is genuinely not looking for food of any kind.

It is quite funny to watch when this happens – to someone else, of course.

There they are, either walking or jogging along happily, when they encounter an acquaintance. Instead of moving on with a casual wave or smile, they pause to speak.

After years of research, I have discovered that this is the only way to outsmart the Chennai mosquitoes!

Then, it happens. You can always tell by the sudden pause, the gulp, the glazed-eye look, and the bout of choking and sputtering, followed by the rather embarrassed pretence all round that this just did not happen. The victims soon move on, gripped by a horrible fear that they have now swallowed something that might have the worst effect possible on some or all of their vital organs.

And you, trying not to laugh, reflect on the strange problems affecting the human condition. ▮

Some enjoy socialising; some seek it, and others have it thrust upon them. And it all adds up to the spirit of have-fun-or-die mandatory to this time of year.

NEW YEAR - ALREADY?

TIME REALLY SEEMS to be on a roll these days.

Seems like only yesterday that festivities heralding 2002 were announced from every bill-board in town. The city wore its brightest lights; and 'Happy' signs blinked on and off all over the skyline.

At least, that was the intention. One assumes that even those rather unfortunate signs with un-cooperative bulbs that resulted in messages like "Hay New ear" meant well.

And here we are – it is that time once again.

It is that time when appearance, food and entertainment become the focus in certain quarters, as tired yet determined party animals get ready for the hectic socialising ahead, grimly ignoring aching backs and grey bags dangling from under their eyes.

It is that time when families prepare for the influx of visitors from all corners of the globe by stocking up on crates of mineral water for all those who once ate masala vadai by the roadside.

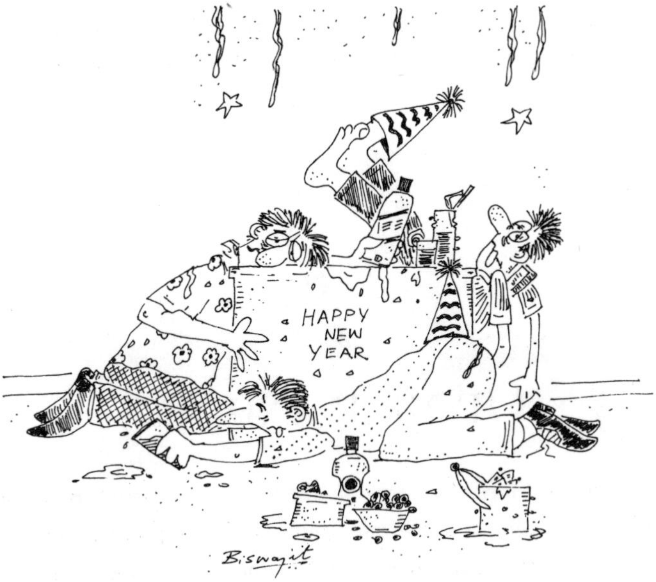

I wonder what's "Happy" about last night!

It is that time to re-make the same list of resolutions that one made, and somehow forgot to keep, last year.

Will December 31st live up to all the anticipation it generates for some?

Hard to tell.

But it is certainly time to wish for happiness and peace on earth for everyone – and really mean it.

The Universe is giving us one more year, after all.

One more chance. ▮

'All creatures great and small' is starting to take on a whole new meaning of late, especially when used in conjunction with the term 'family feeling.'

OF MICE AND MEN

SCIENTISTS (there's no stopping these guys, is there?) recently published almost the entire genetic make–up of the mouse, and this, they say, shows the "animal's startling similarity to people", revealing new insights into Humankind's evolution.

This comes as a slight shock. Just think – while you've been walking around all smug and superior, as befitting those who are supposedly Nature's last word, your close relative has been rushing about squeaking, burrowing holes in gunny sacks and being classified as "vermin." (Well, yes, that might remind you of certain close relatives; and, yes, every family has them…. but - really!)

Scientists, dead-pan as ever, merely call this "interpreting the book of life."

99% of the mouse's genes have counterparts in humankind, including the one that causes tails. (You know, one can't help thinking that maybe some doors should just stay shut.)

However, we don't need to start throwing the word 'family' around immediately as our closest mammal ancestor-in-

Please don't be scared, Amma, they said on TV that man and mouse have a common ancestor… and I have invited my little relatives for a snack!

common existed 75 million years ago, which gives a new twist to the term 'cousin-several-times-removed.' We do come close enough to re-think all those pesticide ads, though.

Incidentally, did you know that a 700-year-old fresco of a medieval rodent, bearing a distinct resemblance to Mickey Mouse has been found on a wall in Malta, in Carinthia Province?

You think old Walt knew something we didn't?

Say cheese! ▮

Add a '2' before each telephone number, orders officialdom, in that breezy manner they have of dispensing orders like they are bestowing favours. And you, muttering darkly, are left with the daunting prospect of updating an entire phone-book.

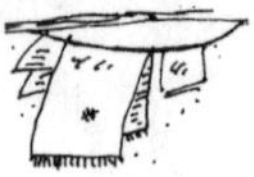

TWO MUCH

POOR CHENNAI-ITES.

Remember that brouhaha – the Number Change – that took place when the powers-that-be decided to issue new door numbers to every residence, causing perplexed citizens to peer doubtfully at their own gateposts to find out what their own house numbers were?

First-time guests, confronted with directions like: "Look for No. 54.... that's new number 54, the old one was 99. Remember...old 54, new 99, no, sorry, the other way around, old 99, new 54..." invariably dropped the idea of a visit and stayed home, opting for either a soul-improving book or cable TV.

Then, just as that tumult settled down, along came the telephone guys, with their version of a bright idea.

"Put a 2 before every number", they intoned.

For creatures of habit (aren't we all?) this creates further forehead furrows. If you forget, a disembodied voice chatters reproachfully at you, reminding you that you've been remiss, causing you to hastily disconnect, cursing freely.

And, let me tell you, there is something darkly surreal about calling one's own residence number and being told it doesn't exist.

You hear some strange conversations.

"My number is 235..., except now, you have to add a 2 so it is 2235...."

"222..."?

"No, just a 2 before the 2...the new 2, followed by the old 2 ..."

For already frayed urban nerves, this sort of jabber results in communication breakdowns, acidity, and lingering headaches.

As if keeping tabs on ever-changing U-turn rules and one-ways aren't tough enough. ▮

First they changed the road names, then the door numbers and now the telephone numbers... thank God, we are the lucky few unaffected by all this confusion!

The vehicle in front of you indicates that it now wishes, for no doubt the best possible reasons, to continue its journey on one of the side-roads so thoughtfully provided. What do you do?

LITTLE SHINING LIGHT

THIS IS FOR THOSE good citizens of Chennai who zip around our wonderful roads using vehicles of various shapes and sizes - especially those who use the two-wheeled variety.

DO YOU KNOW WHAT AN 'INDICATOR' IS?

(I'm sorry – I do apologise for that rather uncontrolled display of emotion.) But I'm sick and tired of drivers careening past your vehicle even as you are in the very act of making a left or right turn.

Indicators, Chennai-ites, indicators.

Pay attention now. Indicators are those clever little lights on the front and rear ends of vehicles. The right one flashes when the driver wants to turn right, and the left one… well, you get the idea.

And when said light blinks, what should you do?

Let the turn go through smoothly, and calmly continue driving. What you do *not* do is suddenly pick up speed, and desperately claw your way through that inch of space between the vehicle-in-the-act-of-turning and the road-corner or whatever the poor guy has to circumvent in order to make that turn.

Honestly, people have had accidents *turning into their own homes* simply because the person behind them decided that the only way he could continue on his journey was by darting between their vehicle *and their own front gate*, ignoring the huge, lovely, empty road on the other side.

We are probably the only country in the world where drivers put their indicators on, and then signal frantically with their hands, twisting this way and that, while fellow passengers lean out of windows yelling instructions ...or expletives.

You have to wonder....who gives people their driving licenses? ▮

I've been walking the Chennai streets for 50 years but am still clueless as to which direction each one is going to turn!

If it is true that all beings, all events, all actions are connected by the threads of destiny, then maybe stepping on every crack in the pavement could help your side win. Touch wood.

Over?

SATURDAY, March 1, '03, post-1.30 pm.

Chennai's roads suddenly emptied, as if a giant hand, wielding a huge sponge, had wiped the streets clean of all traffic.

The reason?

The India-Pakistan confrontation at the World Cup.

The result, of course, was thrilling.

I must confess, though, that I had one more reason to be happy.

I could now leave my chair.

Puzzled?

Well, when cricket-fever hits and Life comes down to TV screens, strange beliefs and superstitions take control of even the most rational of people.

Like, if the going is favourable, then apparently it means you cannot change chairs, for if you move, a match many miles away will be lost. So stay put, even if you are dying of hunger.

If the game picks up when you leave the room briefly, you remain banished till the prize-giving ceremonies are

Not superstitious at all, sir, but we just don't want the luck to change against the Indian team... so, no bath, no shave and no change of clothes till the World Cup is over!

underway. If a much-needed breakthrough occurs when you take a sip of water, you can't put the glass down till the match is over. You feel a distinct tickle in your throat, but cannot cough, as a wicket might fall if you do.

All you can do, therefore, is develop a low throbbing headache, and grimly reflect on the price any all-consuming passion extracts.

So make yourself comfortable, keep nourishment on hand – it's a long haul to March 23rd, 03. ▮

Nostalgia, they say, "isn't what it used to be".
Why bother with old dwellings, then?

KNOCK 'EM DEAD!

IT IS HARD to be an old building in Chennai these days.

Let your walls peel paint; let a little brick-work show; a crack here, a broken window there...and, *whoosh*.... you are history.

Not with a venerable capital 'H', unfortunately.

You cry in vain; you tell people that you've lived in their city from the time when what they now call the past was still a bright, clean present. Many seasons have trailed their fingers along your walls. You have watched Life come, linger, move on, return. You have heard the voice of the city change. You ask people to look at you and see themselves, awaken to a sense of a continuing thread, linking lives. You tell them to look up words like 'heritage' in the dictionary.

Nothing works.

They chase you with bull-dozers and other sharp instruments, intent on tearing you down and having you replaced. The fact that it isn't always commerce or merely the inexorable march of Time which dictates such measures makes it even worse.

Didn't you say he saw the heritage building being demolished?... mmm, he is suffering from SADS – Severe Acute Demolition Syndrome!

Old buildings today are a scared lot, reduced to trembling fear, looking over their shoulders, trying to find shadowy places where they can hide.

(A little like when you were a school kid, and hadn't done your homework. With nothing to offer, you hoped that the teacher's baleful eye would pass you by, descending instead on the class-mate next to you.) ▮

News Flash – the word 'conservative' is no longer attached at the hip to the word 'Chennai', if the new breed of grandmothers in the city is anything to go by.

PIZZA, PAATI?

SCHOOL UNIFORMS, school buses, heavy school bags and lunch boxes.....all regular city sights that have now disappeared on their summer break.

Meanwhile, waves of grandparents meet waves of grandchildren, as families get together.

If that puts you in a maudlin, sentimental mood, going so far as to conjure up a calendar art image of a white-haired, story-telling old grandmother, checked sari et al, making bakhshanam over a kerosene stove, think again.

The bakhshanams are still there, the stories are there and the common enemy – namely the parents – placed squarely as always in the line of fire. The image however has altered slightly, thanks to a certain brand of Chennai's Contemporary Paatis.

These feisty ladies share nail polish and go on beauty parlour dates with their granddaughters and discuss the rival merits of WWF and NWA with their grandsons. They compete for home computer time with their grandchildren,

Summer camps are great for upgrading your skills...
one never knows what will come in handy in one's old age!

and have cute e-mail IDs. They argue whether Harry Potter is better than Lord of the Rings, and have definite opinions on that young Khan's way of 'doing' his hair.

This brand of Paati can cook up a smashing spicy paneer roll with the same aplomb with which she tosses up a sepangkilangu varuval, or create a divine dark chocolate and mint mousse with the same unruffled efficiency with which she makes her famous badam halwa.

And – the more things change, the more they stay the same. ▮

Spare a thought for the techno-phobe, as he and others of his ilk languish in the outer darkness, shuddering at the sight of an instruction manual, and gazing yearningly at the rest of humanity rejoicing in their techno-savvy.

RING-A-RING-A-PULSE-RATE

IUC, WLL, GSM, CDMA, 'basic', 'cellular' - they forgot "incomprehension" and "resultant hyperventilation".

There was a time when the mighty telecom industry was represented, at least for the general mass of humanity, by this standard li'l old black instrument.

Things have certainly changed since those days. Given the level of tech-knowledge, memory skills and infinite capacity for constant mental up-dating now required, those of us who belong to the 'Order of Those-Who-Don't-Get-It' are forced to live with a constant question-mark poised over one's head, and total humiliation. Well-meaning souls try hard to explain these concepts to us. But they soon give up, defeated by the open mouth and blank stare. Unfortunately for the W-m-s, civilised behaviour frowns upon acts of violence against those who haven't been provided with the required number of little grey cells.

Sir, before you start using this cutting edge phone, please read the simple 1000 page instruction manual!

Frankly, methinks there's too much learning in the air.

As for cost involved.... spare a prayer for those who are blessed with cell-phone happy, telephone-addicted teenagers.

We've heard of wise people whose words are 'worth their weight in gold'. Today, that could mean a simple 'hi', for even that comes with a hefty price tag...especially if you are a land line talking to a cell phone. (Or is it the other way around?) This could change the very pattern of greeting, from a friendly 'hello' to a brusque 'Okay, how much is this going to cost me?'

Smoke signals, anyone? ∎

*Behold Chennai's very own personal disaster – being chosen as the only city in the country (that's right, in the **country**) for the 'you-need-a-set-top-box-for-cable-TV-watching' ruling.*

THE IDES OF JULY

IT JUST DOESN'T pay to be on the list of Fate's Chosen Few.

Which is exactly how Chennai was suddenly faced with the prospect of having their Cable TV-watching governed by a small, but very deadly, instrument – the set-top-box.

Poor Cable TV watchers – talk about being ground to dust by the grim heel of Fate.

First, they get tossed around thanks to warring cable-operator factions.

And now, apparently, their destiny was to be ruled by little boxes.

"You are so lucky," the powers-that-be gushed, "You'll get so many channels free." Then, lowering their voices, they added: "Er… you'll have to pay for a few, of course." What they forgot to mention was that all the popular channels had, by some remarkable coincidence, landed on the must-pay-to-watch list.

Cable operators, attempting to oust competition, turned the Cable World into a raucous market-place, where voices argued and bargained.

The big question was: what was one to do?

Buy the box, sniff out the best deals, deposit cash wherever and whenever necessary, and watch your shows uninterrupted? Or eschew the whole mess, and go back to the world of books, conversation, and re-establishing contact with long-forgotten relatives?

Tough call, wasn't it?

Every TV-watching home was poised on the brink of war as the time to make choices from amongst the channels drew near.

As if life isn't complicated enough already.

Gives you some idea of how a fish feels upon finding itself on the wrong end of a fishing rod.

And all because it allowed itself to be tempted. ∎

The only thing positive about the set-top box is that it always brings my boys, Murugan and Kumaran, very "close"!

Perhaps the authorities who dispense driving licenses with the happy insouciance of a monarch flinging largesse to the masses should shift attitudes, and become steely-eyed, talking-through-the-sides-of-their-mouths toughies who mean business.

JUNGLE PATROL

CHENNAI HAS decided to form road safety patrols - 25,000 of them.

It is but only to be expected - citizens who get tired of promised 'solutions' that remain supremely conspicuous by their absence, tend to take matters into their own hands.

While you doff a cap at the effort, you can't help but reflect that these patrols have their work cut out for them.

A patrol, by definition, makes sure people abide by rules… assuming they know them. Therein lies the snag.

Present road usage indicates that our good people are unburdened by any such knowledge. They are free spirits who have turned a certain local expletive into a fact…they really believe the roads are "their grandfather's property".

The patrols will have to be teachers before becoming monitors, dispensing basic lessons.

Leaning on the horn at traffic signals does not make the colours change faster. There is a reason why drivers signal left and right turns. A two-lane should not suddenly develop extra limbs, especially near the signal. The vehicle in front

Jumping traffic lights was the first violation, then parking here was another... now, can you at least show me your license and insurance papers?!

of you has stopped for a good reason, so try not to shoot around him. Speed limits, one-ways and designated U-turns are not just fun concepts.

A road is merely a means of getting you from one place to another. It is not an arena for you to show how much better you are than everybody else.

Let the lessons begin. ▮

Imagine this. Every time you flick a switch, light floods the room – and this pattern never changes. Imagine essential services being dependable 24/7. But how dull.

ELECTRICITY

Light of our lives

Do you believe that a dash of uncertainty adds spice to life, and prevents boredom?

Then the rather whimsical, now-you-see-it-now-you-don't antics of the city's electricity supply must seem exciting to you.

Each day begins with a sense of "Hmmm – I wonder what fun things the power supply has in store for us today".

Chennai's electricity has a way of vanishing - suddenly, devastatingly, and almost always at the worst possible time. Like crucial moments of disclosure on your favorite TV show. Or when you, having tenderly put together several magic ingredients in the mixie, are all set to create a culinary marvel. Or when the most difficult, most critical group of relatives drops in.

Nervous hostesses include short prayers requesting uninterrupted power supply on their "must-do" lists while planning social events.

How about those times when electricity deliberately takes on an alien life form, described rather dully as "voltage

No madam, the power failure in your house is due to our transformer and has nothing to do with the blackouts in New York and London!

problems" by the givers and the givees? Lights grow so dim, all navigation is by instinct. Or they flicker so erratically that your eyes continue to perform a shimmying dance long after supply is restored. This, while headache-inducing, adds interesting dimensions to everyday faces.

And those much advertised perfect wattage bulbs that you took so much trouble over end up looking like asthmatic candles.

Who says essential services have no sense of humour? ▮

The entire weight of a single person's hope-filled ambitions hangs by such a slender thread, depending so much on chance, and the whims and fancies of strangers. And yet, Humanity dares to dream.

OUTWARD HO!

IT IS TIME for the annual visa-rituals to get underway once more, and for the forces of Chance and Destiny to begin their unpredictable, and sometimes deadly, dance.

Just as one set of parents heaves a sigh of relief after having got their young hopefuls into some, or any, college, another begins a long vigil with mixed emotions - hope struggling with the daunting prospect of partially or wholly empty nests.

Everyone's talking countries, colleges and combinations of courses.

Which direction do you choose to travel? Do you apply to some or several schools? Why is the mere process of application so costly? And the weightiest question.....will you get "Aid"? Suddenly, names of states and counties in far off lands spill merrily and confidently from local lips – a situation that appears particularly funny in the case of those who are still pre-disposed to label cuisine from our very own neighbouring States as 'unfamiliar'. With 'virtual visits' now being the norm, surreal, astral-plane

I hope this will be enough to convince them to issue me a visa!

conversations describing campuses and hostel rooms in detail abound.

Long queues begin to snake outside embassies while faces reflect a hope that someone in there will say: "Welcome."

Those of us who have reached the stage of not having to worry about waist sizes or future prospects dreamily recall a certain charming twinkley-eyed performer, who once sang:

"Thank God, I'm not young anymore." ■

Road-rage, best exemplified by pungent diatribes involving the antecedents and mud-like contents of the 'brains' of perceived perpetrators, is showing a marked decrease. Music does soothe the savage beast.

Tuning In

So you thought happy motorists in four wheelers, given today's driving conditions, were an extinct species?

Well, there have been reports of such sightings lately - content faces buzzing around smiling, nodding and tapping out rhythms on steering wheels.

If accompanied by others, they excite little comment, the conclusion being an indulgent: "What a nice, friendly group in that car."

If they indulge in such behaviour when alone, of course, some amount of concern is felt by passers-by, who then mutter among themselves, wondering if they ought to give chase, capture this unnaturally feisty being and sit on his head while someone fetches the proper authorities.

There is however absolutely no cause for concern. The Chennai heat has not had its feared effect of frying its citizens' brains. All that has happened is that people now have something to keep their minds buoyant while driving, thanks to all these bubbly radio stations that have hit the air waves.

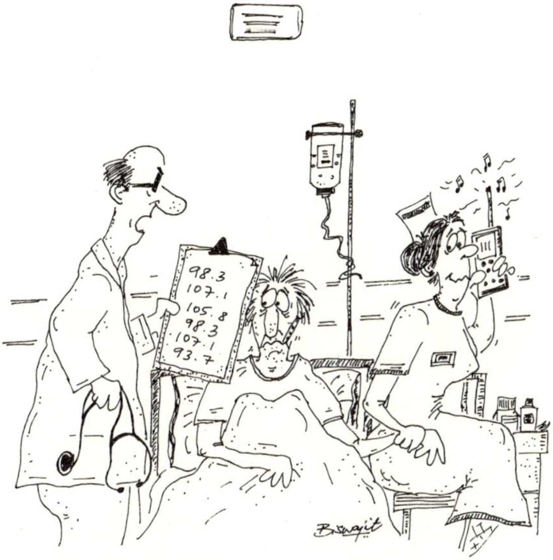

Nurse, I asked you to record the temperature of the patient and not the FM stations you have been listening to!

With sunny, spicy zest, zany characters and talented mimicry, they've succeeded in putting the smile back on at least some of the faces of the battered road-users.

This also means people have less time to stick their heads out of cars, generously tossing around those delightfully acerbic Chennai-isms which have so far been the citizen's only way of expressing emotion while driving – a welcome side-effect. ■

The citizens have been called upon to store essentials, not for a rainy day, but for those scorching dry days. Common sense is not extinct. It merely lurks shyly in the shadows, waiting to be drawn out.

LISTEN TO THE FALLING RAIN

ALL MOTHERS HAVE had the experience of taking that one look too many at their off-spring, and wondering whether it would be possible to exchange the youngsters for a better and cleverer species if they took them back now.

Mother Nature must have felt this way many times, especially as she watched us, for years, let rain water into the sea because we just didn't know what to do or where to stash it.

Hopefully, she's feeling a little better now. Her children have finally woken up, slapped their foreheads and said: "Of course! That is what we should have done in the first place."

House and building owners are diligently scrambling around, with many dwellings now resorting to hanging announcements on their gates and other areas of prominent visibility that they have organized RWH – rainwater harvesting, to the information of the very few who still do not know.

We kept in mind the issue of rainwater harvesting and we came up with this design for your house!

So that's the new status symbol.

About time.

The fact that the authorities wielded a whip and set a deadline has helped galvanise a citizenry inclined to be laid back even about the most impending of disasters.

Those who do not pitch in stand in danger of becoming a hissing and a by-word in socially-aware circles.

All we have to do now is look at the sky and await the deluge. ∎

Ah, Chennai's coastline. If only one could fling one's head back, let the sea breeze dance through one's hair, without fear that one's feet would become hopelessly entangled in someone else's idea of afternoon tea.

Clean sweep

A CERTAIN NEWS item appeared a while ago, indicating that our beaches are being cleaned up - by a special machine, no less.

Good thing too.

It is hard to appreciate the grandeur of Nature when one is skipping delicately from foot to foot, trying to avoid sharp shards of glass, plastic and other reminders of the passage of human hordes through the ages. Running prettily like a movie-star through teasing waves at the very edge of the sea is all very well – except that one is in constant danger of tripping over a half-hidden broken bucket-handle and performing the somersault of a life-time.

Such dangers are now past.

Joggers, walkers, and amblers can now look straight ahead as they go along, giving their neck muscles a rest from watching the ground at their feet. Family parties need no longer warn their uncaring progeny about 'dirty sand'; the romantically-inclined can focus on matters of importance, undisturbed by wandering flotsam (or jetsam?); while

It will only take a few minutes, saar, we have to make sure that the beach is kept clean at any cost!

the artistically-inclined can wrestle with their muses to their hearts' content without having the process broken by the sharp jabs of intrusion.

One understands many lakhs will be spent in this exercise, making this one expensive way to learn not to litter.

So, the next time your hand goes into throw-mode on the beach – pause and reflect. ▮

The clamour of a million voices that come at you, claiming to have stumbled upon the elixir of how-to-stay-thin-with-minimum-effort, softens to a murmur for a day.

SWEET SEASON

WELL, DEEPAVALI HAS come – and gone, and the city sits back, exhausted after the frantic shopping, the clogged roads outside equally clogged shops, the buying and bursting of crackers, (almost inevitably accompanied by anti-burn ointments, band-aids, and adult admonitions.), topped off by the restless behaviour of umpteen boxes of sweets and dry fruits whizzing around the city, flying in and out of homes and offices. Watching them, one wonders if it makes better sense to set up committees a few weeks before the festival to decide who sends what, to avoid danger of repetition. There's something a little farcical about two homes exchanging the exact same burfi, contained in gift boxes that look alarmingly alike.

A question arises – given today's obsessive emphasis on fitness and the eternal-slim-look, are Deepavali sweets looked at with critical severity, making them feel forlorn and neglected, longing for the days when Grand-Aunt X, clueless about cholesterol, didn't care that every diamond-cut cashew kathali was going straight to her hips and waist?

Your weight gain is normal, sir… you have succumbed to what we call the sweet circle of life!

Do the badam burfis, badhushas and pista rolls now wish they were less rich, so customers would choose them, instead of merely gazing at them longingly from a distance?

No, indicate the crowds at the sweet-shops, proving that some attitudinal changes can be reversed on demand.

It is good to know people haven't forgotten how to take holidays from themselves. ▮

There is obviously a thin line between Fame and Notoriety, and finding your name up on a billboard may not be as wonderful as you think.

WHAT'S YOUR NAME?

LITERARY LEGEND HAS it that Lord Byron woke up one morning and found he was famous.

Well, one assumes that old George Gordon felt suitably gratified and pleased with himself - always a nice state of mind to be in.

A certain king of names currently sitting on brightly coloured billboards all over town is not having that same effect on its many owners though.

Those who have had possession of this name for many years and therefore can justifiably lay early claim to it are feeling just a bit put upon.

"What is this?" they ask. "You couldn't get anything else? You couldn't make up a name? You had to pick ours, albeit in a slightly disguised form?"

This business of high-jacking a name to get the message in your advertisement across raises tricky questions.

Does one have a copyright over one's name?

That can't be me! What are they trying to do? Put a black "dot" on my otherwise spotless reputation?

And would these same people mind their name being used for, say, an exotic perfume? Or the smash hit movie of the year, maybe?

Rumour has it that a new underground movement is on. "King's Generals", they call themselves, swearing awful oaths under - well, not old oak trees, obviously, but under anything that's a passable imitation - resolved upon revenge.

You steal someone's purse, you may end up with nothing. You help yourself to someone's name, you're in danger of being called a few choice ones yourself. ▮

You know what they say about good intentions.

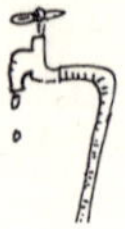

BIG PROBLEMS

RESTLESSNESS IS RIFE amongst a gentle species generously endowed in both body and heart - the domesticated elephants. They are a disturbed lot today, prone to sudden mood changes and a general ennui. Lower lips are in pout-mode, and the sound of occasional rumbling grumbling has been reported.

This is only natural. Anyone who has been away on a holiday will tell you that the post holiday getting-back-to-routine phase is both painful and traumatic.

(Example - Monday mornings.)

Things got pretty exciting for these jumbos in the recent past, when around 55 elephants were sent away for a spot of R&R in the Nilgiris. First, the pachyderms had to cope with the surprise of having humans behaving like - well - human beings. Nothing in their previous experience had given them any reason to believe that this particular species was capable of thinking of anyone else but themselves.

We shouldn't have sent him to that rejuvenation camp at Ooty... see, now he is demanding a manicure, a pedicure, a facial and a full body massage!

Suddenly, there they were, feted, fussed over, in a distinctly clubby atmosphere, complete with multi-cuisine buffets, and herbal tonics. Then, just as they were getting used to the good life, the holiday was over, and they were hauled back to everyday reality.

No wonder they are upset and disinclined for work.

Anyone who has fed on honey-dew and drunk the milk of paradise needs time to re-adjust.

A holiday to recover from the holiday, in other words. ■

Yechuse me, machi, there's nothing to compare with the character and colour of Madras Bashai – and that's no peela.

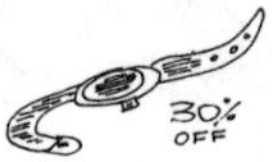

Konjum mixing

Visitors to Chennai are a puzzled lot these days. Apparently, some of those huge hoardings the city delights in are getting them all confused over language issues. (Who isn't – confused, I mean?)

Now this bunch of well-informed people knows the lingua franca of our good old State, is aware of the script, or at least what it looks like.

So naturally, they can't understand a sentence that goes: "Hello Machi, calling attention to Dhool Sale, Ba!" blazoned in brilliant letters across an equally brilliant background.

"Excuse me," they ask tentatively. "What is that?"

"Oh, it's just an advertisement." you reply.

"Yes, we know....but in what language?"

"It's a sort of Tamil."

"Well, we've been all over the State, and we haven't seen anything like that."

"That's because that bashai – 'language' to you uninitiated types – is quintessentially Madras." (Sorry, 'Chennai' just doesn't seem to cut it in this instance.)

They gaze at you, eyes narrowed, then suddenly ask: "What's a 'machi?".

"Oh, just a 'pal'."

"And what's a 'Dhool?"

" 'Super'."

"In what?"

"I told you…in Madras-speak." You are getting rattled, trying to remember that the strict rules of Indian hospitality frown upon dotting an 'athithi' on the head.

"And what's a…."

"Sorry, time to kilambings", you say, rushing off even as puzzled looks dawn.

That's the trouble with these 'peter-parties' – too hidebound, with absolutely no imagination. ▮

It's Tinglish, maamu… konjam Tamil, konjam English!

Ah, how sweet are the memories of the old homestead as you, trapped in peak hour traffic and aging by the minute, inhale the dark emanations that engulf you.

LONG WAY HOME

YOU PACK A BAG with bottles of water, a couple of sandwiches, some biscuits, a good book (remembering at the last minute to toss in reading glasses), and a few paper napkins.

Then, you pick up the bag, and march grimly to your car.

Teeth set, eyes narrowed – you are now in full deal-with-it mode, all set to travel 5 km down the road....*in Chennai's peak hour traffic.*

What has happened to this city? Every road is crammed to the brim with vehicles, exploding at the sides, spilling on to pavements, even informally entering those houses placed a little too close to the street.

As for traffic signals - vehicles nestle together for so long at each one, you can make new friends, start new business ventures, write that novel you've been dreaming about, and possibly even fall in - and out - of love in all that time.

Even the most mundane of journeys requires high-precision planning, with people muttering: "Okay, I go down *this* road, turn left into *that* little lane, so I can avoid *that*

There is nothing abnormal with the lines on your hand.
It's perfectly normal to be stuck in traffic jams…
after all, you are in Chennai!

signal, then make a U-turn *there* (unless they've scrapped it) to avoid the 'movie's-finished' crowd, then….".

The moving traffic clogs, and chugs right on, and not all the flyovers and one-ways will lure clear roads back to ease our lives.

Maybe we citizens should stay home more often. ▌

There are two sides to every story. When the bird-flu scare hit us, did anyone pause to think of the sensibilities of our feathered friends?

FOWL MOOD

SOMEONE UP there seems pretty mad at us.

First, scary SARS that had everyone starting nervously, spinning around with deep suspicion at the sound of a sniff or a sneeze.

And now this bird-flu - the latest Mexican-wave of panic and doubt to engulf the world.

It has unfortunately changed the way one regards a fellow species. Our feathered fowl friends in Chennai are in a disgruntled mood, one hears. They have so far been used to eliciting certain stock responses from most viewers, who either go "Awww, how chweet" or "Yuummm", depending on individual points of view... (and no, we are not getting into any debates here.) Of course, a fairly large chunk of the populace has no strong feelings either way, and will inform you rudely enough that they have better things to do with their time, thank you very much, should you press for an opinion.

But now, the chick-brigade is beginning to feel discriminated against. Hitherto opposite schools of thought are suddenly united in looking askance at them, they say,

I know the lab tests have come out negative, but I should still think that it is bird flu virus!

adding that their lot is tough enough without being slandered like this.

The general feeling is that they should be judged as individuals and not clubbed together with their unfortunate brethren in other parts of the world, sorry as they are for them.

"Use common sense." they urge.

Ah, there's the problem. ▮

It's an ants-thing, rushing here and there, filling every moment, because you cannot risk staying still. It seems it is never too early for kids to learn the old "Life is real, life is earnest..." adage.

WAS SCHOOL OUT FOR SUMMER?

FIRST SIGN OF approaching summer holidays these days – brightly coloured banners springing up, promising "exciting, innovative, fun-filled *learning* experiences" for children supposedly on vacation.

The city was recently drowning in an abundance of such 'camps'.

First off, I really doubt if kids were conned by big smiling adults who combined the words 'learning' and 'fun' in the same sentence. They knew this for what it was - not so much "Camp-Summer-fun" as "Camp-let's-get-the-pesky-kids-out-of-the-way."

Little tykes, (and some not so little), were packed off in different directions, fervently assured that they would "have a great time and make lots of new friends."

I don't know – did anyone bother to ask them if they wanted so much fun thrust down their throats...or even felt the need to "make lots of new friends"?

I'm telling you for the hundredth time, this was not my idea of fun… my mom told me it would be fun and I believed her!

Admittedly, long summer holidays are tough, with kids home 24/7, while parents deal with unsympathetic work spots that refuse to see school holidays as an excuse for adults goofing off. Out of town options are subject to time and economics. But when kids are not offered the option to just 'be' - even in the summer - you can't help feeling just a bit sorry.

If one can be forgiven tampering with the words of an immortal song from another era, one would say:

"Hey, people, leave those kids alone". ▮

Where the mind is without fear...... of imagination.

A LITTLE BIT OF THIS, A PINCH OF THAT

'COMBINATION' - THE dreaded buzz-word in homes with children of a certain age group.

"Finished tenth? What combination next year?" is the terse question addressed to parents and teenagers alike, to the confusion of the uninitiated.

Homes reverberate to arguments and endless discussions, with scary words like 'future prospects' flung at the poor child's head. But how does one look for all-round solutions among such unrelentingly tight combinations of subjects?

If you choose one that interests you, you find to your horror that several others leap to their feet, insisting that you take them too.

If you like to study plants, you also have to wrestle with numbers. That's tough on those who (like me) never cared when two trains, travelling in opposite directions, one serving rava dosai and the other vadai-chutney, would cross each other.

This scientific exercise will help Ramu choose the right group for his Plus-2… shouldn't be a blind choice, you see!

Imagine being stuck for a couple of years with stuff that leaves you cold, just to study the one subject you want. Imagine what that does to you, your academic performance. Imagine…. Ah, if only the powers-that-be had a little more of that…. (!!!)

Are there any fun combinations out there – like Mathematics with Fine Arts; or Chemistry with Literature; or Physics with Music?

Fun – maybe that's the lesson being taught here. That real life is not fun.

How sad and dreary is the path we shoo our children on. ▌

The mere act of winning does not seem to guarantee congratulations based on trust. Maybe there's a good reason why some people are scared of success.

You just can't win

Imagine this.

Two teams, both having given a great deal of thought to matters of grave concern such as selection of individual members and general strategy, confront one another on the battlefield of sports.

As usually happens on such occasions, one team wins.

And having done so, they find, much to their consternation, that many who have lost their voices yelling themselves hoarse in support, and perhaps their jobs in some instances on charges of goofing off, are now chewing their lips in doubt and going: "Hmmm." in an ominous way.

One can only begin to guess at the emotional state of a winner who shuffles up, laden down with diverse medals and trophies, in happy anticipation of kudos, only to stub his toe on a 'that's-all-very-well-but-did-you-win-fair?' attitude.

And that too from the one source he thought was completely on his side, urging him on with word and gesture.

Our school won the cricket match, Appa…
and believe me, it wasn't fixed!

How strange are the workings of the human mind.

We grasp failure to ourselves with an almost welcoming fervour, wallowing in subsequent martyrdom, with endless hours being devoted to blame allocation and angry analysis.

But success we view with suspicion; either embarrassed by it, or wondering if the path leading to it was….er…. subjected to some amount of "help".

One can't help feeling a bit sorry for the heads that wear these uneasy crowns. ▮

SMS-ing and the art of communicating with your kids.

U R 2 MUCH

IT'S BEEN A while since adults made eye-contact with the spring-time-of-their-lives generation. This is largely because the latter are either constantly looking at the palms of their hands, or holding a ear, as if fearing that this useful attachment will suddenly take flight unless battened down thus.

And the reason for these strange goings-on?

The getting-tinier-and-more-complex-by-the-minute, ubiquitous cell phone.

Isn't it amazing how children who display abysmal motor skills while cleaning their rooms have no trouble sending SMS messages, fingers moving with manic, yet unerring, speed – *without once looking at the keys?*

They also conduct simultaneous conversations – one courteous and verbal; and the other silent and rather unique in its use of letters.

If it isn't messages, it is games, played on this combination of mere communication tool and unbelievably sophisticated toy.

As for that 'Down-load ring tones' stuff - only people whose fond children have 'down-loaded' tunes expressing emotions slightly inappropriate to the formers' discreet age and (presumed) venerable wisdom, know the meaning of the term 'feeling foolish'.

What's worse, with so many adults still being a little techno-challenged, too frightened to attempt to access even voice-mail for instance, there's not a thing to be done except wait for the pesky kids to come back from wherever, and restore respectability by changing the ring-tone to something more ordinary, albeit a little dull.

Incidentally, all this adult tut-tutting merely proves that scoffing and pretending disinterest has always been the mature way to deal with inferiority complexes. ∎

What a wonderful present he's got for his first birthday! Now, he can watch video clips, play games, download songs, take pictures, send SMS to all his friends with his own cell phone!

Question: What's worse than finding a worm in an apple?
Answer: Finding half a worm in an apple.
That goes for chocolate too.

BURROWING IN

IT IS A FACT that there are many new-fangled diets in vogue these days, suggesting unusual combinations of food groups to ensure that slim school-kid look. You can't open a newspaper or magazine without running into column after column filled with the eat-right, weigh-right, feel-right sort of guilt-inducing information.

But worms in chocolates?

Now that was a shocker. And that too from a brand that's proved trusted and true over generations. It's like finding out that your grandmother leads a secret double life – Gran by day, card sharp by night.

What were those guys thinking? And how did our slithery friends manage to get themselves so snugly and firmly ensconced inside bars and bars of chocolate, escaping initial detection?

After that scare, parents began to watch their off-spring in guilty fear, wondering how many of the creepy-crawlies their young ones had feasted on in the recent past.

Oooh – the horror.

Those enterprising worms, of course, must have been a richly happy lot. Having drawn a slightly short-ish straw in the evolution stakes, they've grown accustomed, over centuries, to being shuddered at, squealed at, rejected, destroyed, and being treated, in short, like worms.

And then – came the dawn. Attention, TV coverage, magazine and newspaper articles – talk about an Andy Warhol moment. All this while being able to dip themselves thoroughly, decadently, in loads of dreamy, yummy chocolate.

However, there was a flip side, and the unhappy humans in charge of chocolate-bar production were enmeshed in it, buried under tons of blame, recrimination, and damaged reputations.

Where were the early birds when you needed them? ▮

Please enter the contest and you can find out if you will be the lucky one... to get the worm!

Green hair? Does that mean you now have to get a whole new wardrobe to match? What fun.

HAIR RAISING

THE HUMAN RACE'S valiant (and sometimes quaintly conceited) efforts to improve upon the charms Nature bestowed upon them are never-ending.

They cut, snip, add, subtract, paint – anything to achieve the Body Beautiful, and get the better of a mischievous fate that, uncaring of personal ambition, invariably, and unkindly, orders that a strong resemblance to an experiment in an old Gothic novel be one's lot.

For a while now, it's been open season on crowning glories, proving that our good citizens too display this naïve belief in their ability to outsmart natural law.

The powers-that-be had once decreed that the sub-continent generally grew heads of dark brown to black hair. A decade ago, the prospect of a parrot-green head of hair gamboling up the steps of certain much-respected, age-old centers of culture and tradition (that had hitherto only seen dark, sometimes severely oiled, hair juxtaposed with reams of jasmine strands), was unthinkable.

Not any more.

Hair colouring for me, perm for my daughter and hair bonding and ironing for my grandmother!

We now have heads of hair displaying a range of colours that runs the gamut of a child's painting box – discreet strands in some cases; thick tumbling locks in others. Multiple contrasting colours share one head with ease, and purple nestles alongside shocking pink or blue, surrounded by natural black.

What now?

Education/work places setting rules on 'acceptable' colours?

Matrimonial ads adding 'great hair colour' to that strange list of attributes, starting with 'Tall, fair' etc? ▮

The grandparents wouldn't mind a touch of Thai; the middle generation wishes to check out the latest fusion-food in town; the kids are clearly, and loudly, for impossible-to-maneuver, thickly-layered foot-long sandwiches. Stale-mate.

GUESS WHO'S...(SORRY!) *WHERE* WE'RE GOING FOR DINNER?

HERE'S A PIECE of advice to all those who are about to begin work on the construction of new homes – Do not bother building kitchens.

This applies to both individual homes and those that shoot brightly to the sky over the ruins of old buildings, ignoring a couple of small, sad ground-bound facts – lack of parking facilities, and depleting water tables.

Seriously though, don't waste time and creativity trying to carve out unique hearts-of-homes. A small counter and a couple of shelves will suffice.

For, judging by the crowds that throng to restaurants of all shapes, sizes, cuisines and price-ranges, and by the number of food supply outlets that have mushroomed all over, Chennai prefers to dine out these days.

Oh, they're only waiting to be seated at your table, but don't let that bother you, sir... just relax and enjoy your meal!

Home cooking may have to be declared an endangered form of social activity, while standing around in restaurants waiting for a table, and trying to guilt those who are already dining into hurrying up, is becoming common practice.

This movement gained momentum when the last bastion fell. When the generation that traditionally sniffed in contempt at 'outside food' discovered the joys of fast food and other myriad delights of the gastronomical kind, old eating habits, including the grim tenacity with which fixed meal times were once adhered to, collapsed with a final groan. Three generations tumbling out of one vehicle, arguing vociferously about what to eat is quite a common sight today.

One side effect - Some of that bequeathed kitchenware is starting to look distinctly cobwebby, and appears to have grown roots. ▮

Room for one? You'll have to take the whole bunch - and then some.
We are like this only.

NINE'S A CROWD

IT HAS BEEN reported that a certain brand of public transport is showing signs of disgruntled restlessness, feels alienated, discriminated against, and wants to stand up and be counted.

And therein lay the problem.

Apparently some official did do a spot of counting and found one too many heads in said transport system, resulting in a certain amount of tut-tutting, with rule books being quoted and laws laid down sternly.

Obviously, safety precautions are paramount. Crowding and foot-board travel are sources of major anxiety, both for the travellers, and those vehicles that follow closely behind. It is equally imperative that commuters get all the help they truly need.

But if a slightly different dimension may be brought in here: There really is no point in asking members of this sub-continent to travel in smaller numbers.

We like to travel in packs, live in a crowd. That's why one lone traveller is always seen off by something that resembles a small European nation.

No, the dog is not man's best friend, but who will share my thoughts?!

A family outing is a laudable exercise, certainly, but who decides the size of the family among people who consider a neighbour's third cousin by marriage a close friend and relative, practically a sibling?

We define a two-wheeler as ideal transport for a family of four, or even more, if a couple of members are shrimp-sized.

It is probably easier, and safer, to make modes of transport in large economy sizes. ■

If all that comes out of an open tap is a gurgle, a hiccup and a puff of dust, attempts to make the populace focus on the 'bright' side could lead to justifiable mayhem.

தண்ணீர்

SUMMERTIME – AND THE LIVIN' IS EASY?

IT IS HERE – just as predicted – and dreaded.

The Absolutely-No-Water crises, worsening day by day, in a 'shining' land where the future looks so bright, you can't get a bucket of water.

This havoc-riddled situation contains endless avenues for trouble and strife – and certain not-so-obvious spin-offs.

Like its effect on the age-old traditions of hospitality, for instance.

The old 'honoured guests' philosophy will be re-thought in Chennai this summer.

Under normal circumstances, most hosts watch with self-congratulatory pride as their guests feed well at the table. But now, it will be more like: "Eat all you want, people, but not more than two sips of water each."

Not the sort of attitude that makes for social conviviality.

Extended families living away that begin long-distance telephone conversations with a cheerful: "Hi, we thought we'd spend the summer with you guys." will wonder if they've got the wrong number, as a distinctly doubtful, embarrassed silence floats back over the line.

There are ways out, though – guests can always be told to bring their own buckets and independently organised sources of water.

What will the citizenry do?

Hold on tight, and grimly await solutions and better days in some dim future.

And look up at the relentlessly bright blue sky – searching for answers.

They've become experts in the art of hoping anyway, over the years. ▮

Oh no, we are not travelling by train or car… we are going by this water tanker to Chennai for our holidays!

The following line must be sung:

How many children must grow up confused, before we adults…
(in a rush) get-our-act-together?
(Long Pause…) Allright, one tried to set that line to a certain famous tune; it didn't work out - the words refused to fit. Moving on…

WANTED: A PIED PIPER

ONE CAN'T SPEAK for the adults in this country, but one has to hand it to the children here. They are a wonderful, patient, trusting lot, displaying constant faith in the adults ruling their lives – a faith that said adults do everything they can *not* to live up to.

Witness the chaos over all these various 'entrance' exams, for instance.

Traditionally, by the time the dreaded season for these exams rolls around, parents and children are worn out with the sheer effort of wading through foggy mists of contradictory information, trying to take effective decisions (that include dreams as well) in the process.

It's hard enough picking which examination to take; which one to ignore…...

And now a fresh bogey has raised its head:

There are no guarantees whether said examination will have any relevance at all when the time comes for seats to colleges be allotted.

How crazy is that?

You can stop writing now... I've just been informed that the college has scrapped this entrance exam!

Children go through endless trauma and stress to somehow achieve as-it-is absurdly high percentages, only to have some rule-making adult state with studied nonchalance: "Er...you know that series of exams you took a while ago? Well, actually, those results do not count anymore. Sorry. Too bad."

The need of the hour: a gentle, wise Pied Piper, to pipe children to a better world, where their minds are free from fear; untouched by the actions of goofy adults. ▮

Sometimes there are rhymes and reasons – time-tested ones, at that - for the way things are.

Shenanigans on the Banana Leaf

Good old *yellai sapad* – tried and trusted formula, traditionally used at all meal-times during any celebratory occasion pretty much all over the South. A given set of known dishes, served in a prescribed order as comfortingly familiar as the aroma of one's Grandma's attempts at making bakshanam.

Or so it was.

There have been some strange goings-on for a while now in the land of *yellai sapad* design, resulting in people asking a question that never ever needed to be asked in days of not-so-yore:

"*What comes next*?"

Now, one isn't against change; or so hide-bound that one can't accept it in a spirit of good-humoured tolerance.

But, with all due respect to world cuisine, when a strange, (and hybrid) form of Far Eastern noodles slithers into one's puliogarai, it creates a dazed feeling of "Where-am-I?"

Vegetable noodles with drumstick sambar and salsa sauce...
a rather unique combination, but very tasty!

Likewise upon discovering something that's a cross between a doughnut and a janghiri.

The sight of a quintessential wedding guest trying to wolf down 'Gobi Manjurian Dry' (one has seen it spelt that way – honest) in conjunction with sambar sadam, while wistfully dreaming of good old potato roast, takes you into a strange, surreal world.

Change, they say, is 'as good as a feast'. Perhaps – but do quests for originality sometimes get just a bit feverish? A mild – very mild – touch of 'a-time-and-place-for-everything' isn't always a limiting concept. ■

When you lean against your wall, and find a strange unwillingness on its part to support you, it's time to re-think your present choice of city.

Falling down

Perfect.

The good citizens of Chennai have not only to worry about water shortages, congested roads, being the only ones in the country dealing with the Great Set-Top-Box Experiment, searing heat and humidity that puts a damper on everything – they now have to look at their buildings in a spirit of fear and distrust.

Certain brainy folks have discovered that Chennai's structures are more prone to corrosion than one would wish, rendering them shaky and therefore just a bit undependable.

You know that strange sense of things being a little skewed that you've been experiencing? It may not be merely the result of too many late nights.

It isn't only buildings; it is vehicles as well, especially those that haven't received that crucial coat of anti-corrosion paint. Imagine bowling cheerily down Anna Salai in peak traffic, only to have your vehicle collapse around you with a loud and embarrassing clang.

You are right, there was a first floor,
but you see, the corrosion has...

And there's not much you can do about all this, except probably give the Bay of Bengal a dirty look, because it appears this is typical of coastal areas, especially when combined with frenetic industrial and urban activity.

So there you have it.

The next time you make that dramatic exit from your home, don't slam the door.

The statement 'roof over one's head' might turn out to be just that, in a rather more drastically literal sense. ■

They provide the day, tell you of the occasion, and even teach you the emotion that goes with it. Clever, clever people.

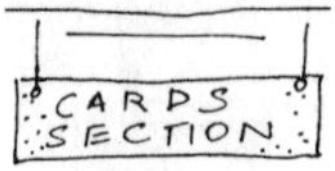

JUST ANOTHER DAY IN PARADISE

365 DAYS IN a year, right?

No arguments there, not even from those who have uniquely individual attitudes with regard to perception of time.

Now some of these days have, over the years, acquired identities for themselves, evolved into 'Days' with a capital 'D', so to speak – festivals, holidays, historical landmarks, days symbolic of the ebb and flow of life, some good, some sad, some ethnic, some global...you get the picture.

But it seems of late that there are just a bit too many days clamouring for attention, allotting themselves labels, insisting that they too be counted as 'Days' – and celebrated.

Bit suspicious that, with a distinct sense of "Hmmm-I-wonder-now" being directed towards those engaged in the gift-and-card trade – all respectable and wonderful citizens no doubt, but whose business conferences probably go like this:

Big Boss: *Well, any ideas? Come on, come on, speak up.*

Obsequious underling: *Yes Sir. We thought we'd designate the 15th two months from now as Chewing Gum Recycling Day. Here are the prototypes of the cards, posters, mugs, T-shirts, and wrist-bands. Here's the jingle we've composed. And, oh yes, the media has been alerted and are all set for the blitz.*

Big Boss, (wiping emotional tears): *Carry on the good work, people. Carpe Diem and all that...literally.*

Cynical?

Probably.

And yet: Why blame the think-tank guys when the world proves such an easy, willing victim? ▮

Can you please help me find a simple "Happy Birthday" card?

Thinkers and creators of the world, be warned.
The world is cruel to those with unique gifts.

Tall tales

We seem to live in touchy times.

At any given point, someone out there is feeling hurt or picked on, demanding apologies, and grumbling about the general rot in society's foundations.

This constant demand to tread lightly is especially tough on those in high visibility professions.

Like script writers, for instance.

Looks like they can't move a step these days without stepping on someone's particularly tender toes, forcing them to either move around like ballerinas dancing on fragile egg-shells, or choose formulae over imagination.

There are entire brigades, mostly self-appointed, slinking around, armed with huge magnifying glasses, ready to pounce on the slightest hint of 'incorrectness'.

Those who use their art to hold a mirror up to society had better choose one that reflects only acceptably pale versions of life, its passions and colours, because, hey, anything else is too close for comfort.

I have a feeling that they are here to tell us that our latest movie has hurt the sentiments of geese all over the world!

No wonder some of them wish they had taken up safer professions, like bull-fighting, or studying king cobras.

The brigades are quite reasonable – they merely request that one avoids all home truths, realities, and even the mildest attempt to laugh at ourselves – anything else is fine.

You know what, guys? Stick to fairy tales, to perfect larger-than-life characters who never have to deal with shades of grey. Bad is bad; good is good, and there's nothing in between.

We like being lied to – it's easier. ▮

Slither and slide; run and hide, for you have the DVD/VCD of this week's Friday release – and it's only Monday.

Skull and cross-bones

He peers through the glass doors, rather like an enquiring tortoise. He glances furtively, this way and that. Is anybody watching?

No, it's all clear. Clutching his booty under a voluminous shawl (*in 38 degrees? That's a dead give-away in itself*), he shuffles hurriedly to his vehicle and drives home. Even his car appears to skulk and crouch. The front door opens a little; he slips through. The windows, draped in thick black cloth, shut out light - and discovery. The small gathering inside greets him silently, raising their collective chins in a silent question. He nods tersely, in silent affirmative. The people cheer – silently. (*There's a lot of silence around, as in all such dark doings*). He approaches the DVD/VCD player, slips in the secret object from under his shawl, then grins as the names of the newest flavour-of-the-month stars explode dramatically on the screen – and, somewhere in the city, various distributors and exhibiters leap out of their already disturbed sleep, sensing they've been done in again.

I'm the only "pirated" version here and everything else is original, I think!

Is it worth it?

Is it so difficult to wait for a (mostly familiar) smorgasbord of song and dance numbers, gory revenge, and happy endings to officially hit the screen?

Look, these guys work hard, in rain and shine, to put a smile on your face.

The least you can do is not pull a 'Captain Hook' or a 'Long John Silver' on them. ▮

Some strange side-effects to the global village syndrome as various worlds collide.

THE MEDIUM'S THE MESSAGE

THE WORLD IS shrinking - no doubt about it, and rapidly, at that. And given the rate at which this process accelerates everyday, the third rock from the sun will soon be the size of a peanut, metaphorically speaking, at least, (if that's the word one wants).

This phenomenon appears to have a few fairly surreal spin-offs, providing new twists to the term 'being connected'.

Like - in advertising.

Ruddy-faced, sometimes light-haired, leg-spinners from far-off lands (okay, fine, off-spinners, pinch-hitters, – or whatever whirling action these heroes use to wreak maximum havoc) now appear on our screen, exhorting us to buy our own home grown products – many of which have little to do with their particular areas of expertise.

Suddenly, these hands across the seas are dancing the garba on our TV sets, riding our bikes, wearing embroidered sherwanis, and looking intensely into our eyes via the screen, as they tell us how to do our shopping.

Strong tooth powder, if you please! Now they will really chew up the Indian team!

Which, apart from the element of novelty, raises one question – everyone knows it pays to advertise, but... well...exactly who's the cleverest of us all in this particular case?

What next?

The world record holder for the most number of wickets taken during Test matches sipping a spoonful of fresh-off-the-stove tomato rasam daintily, and going "Mmmm, just like my....er....*your* grandmother used to make it. Buy 'Kanakambal Instant Rasam Powder' today."?

Now that's globalisation. ■

You want to re-think that precious little crystal glass slipper?
Or that dark chocolate?

GIFT-HORSES

WINTER'S HERE AND we're all set to receive plane loads of relatives who will wing their way home now to renew family ties. (Somehow, the whole procedure is so much easier in tolerable weather, isn't it?)

This process of re-connection has always, for some reason, carried with it an obligation to bring gifts.

And here's where today's non-resident, home-coming relative (or friend) has a problem.

Thirty years ago, even those humble ball-pens you probably bought from the hawker at the corner of Lexington-and-East 46th (or whatever) were received with glad, appreciative cries. Younger family members threw fearful scenes, over-ruling parental embargos and insisting on taking them to school the next day, so they could show off about their relatives who had just come "from foreign".

Unfortunately, in today's world, such gestures merely invoke ill-concealed yawns, or mildly polite smiles of acceptance.

Laddus and Tirunelveli halwa as gifts from New Jersey Halwa Home for family and friends back home in India... gosh! Why didn't we think of this awesome idea before?!

There's very little 'They' can buy for 'The People Back Home' anymore, not even 'different' foodstuff. Firstly, they're mostly available here - for a price. Secondly, the country has suddenly gone all health and appearance conscious. Yes, even Old Uncle Stuff-His-Face, who, in the old days, had to be kept off Krishna Jayanthi bakshanams with a stick, is now disgustingly gym-fit.

Visits to malls that have sprung up where all those family houses once stood merely confirms this grim reality – ain't a whole lot new under the sun no more.

Happy family-ing. ▮

A Name tag – You see it; you read it. But what are you actually getting?

TOIL AND SPIN

THERE THEY SIT, so young it's almost painful.

You can always identify these young professionals by those formidably impressive-looking name tags tossed nonchalantly around their necks.

You can't help thinking that most of them look like it couldn't have been too long ago since their mothers wrote out name tags and pinned them on, so they wouldn't get lost in the mad rush of humanity that's nursery school.

There they sit, so young, yet rich enough to make those who remember how the young Bachchan looked, and who've now toiled through to their 50's and over, mumble:

"I had to work 30 years before I could see even a quarter of what those kids make."

Those tags carry such an aura of 'I've-arrived', one almost misses noticing the exhaustion on these youthful faces, as they buzz around imposing buildings filled with many maze-like corridors, but not too many windows.

But the tags – ah, the tags have become so important to image-enhancement, everybody wants to wear them.

When I joined the company, I thought "24 x 7" was a nice fancy name, but now I understand what it really means!

Employers engaged in not-in-flavor businesses find themselves in a spot, gently trying to point out to their own rebellious employees that a staff of two, sometimes just one, isn't likely to run into identification problems. But this only leads to arguments, wounded feelings, and sulking over the eternal 'why-not-me?' factor.

For the tags we pin upon ourselves is what the outside world perceives, after all. ▮

You think that name is just a bit too heavy for the baby?
He seems to be slowly but surely bending in half.

NAME THAT BABY

"THIS IS PRECISELY why fancy, odd-shaped gifts should be avoided." I remarked, watching a friend struggle to wrap a gift, succeeding more at wrapping herself up instead. "Who's this for, anyway?"

"X and Y's new baby." she replied.

I read the card with the presumption of long friendship. "You've merely said: "To the little one." Don't you know the baby's name?"

My friend looked away, biting her lips.

"I do know." she mumbled.

"Then why haven't you written it?"

"It's bdmbdmbdm."

"Eh?"

"Bdmbdmbdm."

"*What?*"

"Oh, all right," she exploded, "Its 'Jagadwikshyat' – and I don't know how to spell it, or even pronounce it, okay? Don't you dare laugh."

She needn't have worried. I wasn't laughing. Just last week, a young NRI family member told us that she was calling her little one 'Icchudhanva'. (It's a good thing she informed us via e-mail). Incidentally, her older child is 'Vikalinikamba'.

There seems to be a trend of late towards names that wear their cultural history a little heavily.

Sure, we have some of the most musical, meaningful names in the world. However, one should pause before imagination catches fire at their sheer beauty.

Remember – the name has to survive playgrounds, schools, teasing classmates, nicknames, perhaps future fame; it must be suitable for cooing, and more likely being yelled or screamed.

Note: Children rarely forgive their parents' lapses – especially slightly over-enthusiastic ones. ▮

How about 01010101… with a name like that, he is bound to succeed in the computer field!

"I don't care if it's completely made of marble, and some Emperor built it. Not a paisa over Rs 100/-"

What a Bargain

WINTER IN CHENNAI.

Life is significantly less damp, and Old Sol isn't throwing his weight about quite as much. Ergo – it's visitors-from-across-the-seas time again in Chennai.

It is easier to appreciate exotica in balmy weather, after all. The locals are happy too – for obvious reasons.

A recent news item, however, proves that some travellers, welcome as they are, come to our shores slightly under, or mis-informed. Apparently there was a small fracas in a railway compartment over the fact that two enthusiastic, (and delightfully adventurous) foreign nationals attempted to bargain with an attendant over biriyani lunch packets. The attendant, understandably, was stunned. The travellers, equally confused, offered in their defense the explanation that they had been told that bargaining was a major communication channel in India. Sympathetic fellow travellers then explained to the bemused tourists that while the 'Great Indian Bazaar' did indeed exist in all its reputed colour, glory, and smooth attempts to make a quick, extra

Saar, you were the one who wanted a 50% off!

rupee, there are limits to its reach. Meal packets distributed by relevant authorities do not come under its purview, for instance.

There have even been instances of visitors getting into the 'Not-a-paisa-more-than…' spirit in certain reputed departmental stores, until gently but firmly set right by salespeople, much to the amusement of local clientele.

Isn't it about time the nation's tourism department did something about 'foreign' perception of shopping in India? ▮

Give them air – clean air, if you can find it.

WAITING TO INHALE

WE WATCHED IN concern as a familiar car halted in an uncharacteristically wobbly manner, and a friend staggered out.

"What's wrong?"

Clutching his head, he replied: "It's finally happened. A through-the-looking-glass moment. Things are upside down, inside out, back to front, topsy turvy...."

This looked like it could take a while, so we called him to order with a well-administered glass of cold water.

He gasped, spluttered a bit, then explained.

"I just saw a *happy traffic cop.* A cyclist and an auto almost landed beneath a speeding water tanker, which in turn narrowly missed eight cars, one bus and a family of four on a two-wheeler who wore the distinct air of having recently indulged in masala dosais and degree coffee. And guess what? The cop *smiled gently and advised everyone to stay calm and breathe slowly through the nose.*"

The mystery was solved.

They must have filled laughing gas instead of oxygen, sir!

The cop had obviously had his most recent snort of oxygen.

Ever since oxygen dispensers were placed at traffic junctions, there have been sightings of happy cops. Well, if they put a smile on the faces of our long-suffering traffic police, dealing as they do with heat, dust, and the sheer abysmal stupidity of road users, then more power to them.

Hurrah for good old oxygen – even if it has to be offered in dispensers thanks to earnest human efforts to wipe out clean air. ▮

Will Chennai burst out laughing if its citizens complain of feeling chilly?

SHAWL, ANYONE?

CHENNAI-ITES ARE A confused lot these days. For decades, they have been assailed by endless heat and humidity jokes and digs at their city's rather unfortunate weather patterns, all of which they have received with the sportsmanship and good humour they are renowned for.

(No, I'm *not* kidding!).

And now suddenly, Nature, who has always professed to be a creature of habit, has decided to re-work patterns.

I don't know if you've noticed, but it gets a little…er… cold during our 'winters', of late.

The deliberately derogatory term 'ha-ha' that used to be attached to the word 'winter' by non-locals while speaking of the Season in Chennai is slowly losing its sting.

So here's the problem.

Crisp vaishtis, bright sarees and jasmine flowers…. comfortably familiar – even today. But shawls and sweaters?

Chennai-ites are unable to deal with this new image of themselves.

“It has been very, ummm, very *pleasant*, hasn’t it?” they ask each other, closely monitoring reactions to that statement. They are not too sure – are they breaking some unwritten law that a Chennai-ite may only perspire, not shiver?

A mild drop in temperature during these months is common, but an actual bite in the air feels strange.

The citizens are not sure if they are imagining those little quivers and shudders, and feel distinctly foolish to venture out tucked into warm clothing.

Chennai is not used to seeing her citizens bundled up.

Some shops have begun displaying rather gorgeous woolens – unheard of and never-before-seen in Chennai-that-was-Madras.

What does this signify?

That slowly, but surely – the Ice Age cometh once again, perhaps? ▮

You look great and comfortable. I’m very happy I picked it up at the year-end sale… perfect for Chennai winter!

The sign board clearly announces that this road is a one-way, which naturally explains why so many vehicles are travelling merrily along it specifically in the out-lawed direction

FLYING LEAP

SO YOU THOUGHT being a cop would be like something out of a fast-paced, glitzy TV show?

Think again.

Better still, ask those uniformed gentlemen who were recently forced to exchange the heroic for the downright ridiculous, and run after our citizens instead, trying to prevent them from leaping over medians straight into the paths of veritable torrents of traffic.

Does the populace think medians have been placed in the exact centre of busy roads because, after having ordered miles of them on a whim, the authorities didn't know what to do with them?

It's the same questionable thought process that allows people to see, and register, the areas designated as 'pedestrian crossings,' yet deliberately choose to dart across in an uniquely confused, hysterical manner at those unmarked sections of the road teeming with thickest traffic.

There is this reluctance on part of our good people to do as they are told. Gypping our railways out of platform

It was a good leap as usual, but the poor fellow didn't notice that we'd put up a higher road divider last night!

tickets, refusing to circle the circle, (you know what I mean,), ignoring the 'No Horn' sign within hospital compounds – there is something about an established rule that immediately creates an irresistible urge to break it.

We who are so justifiably proud of our history and tradition – wouldn't it be great if we, as a people, also learnt to ...well, stand in orderly queues and wait our turn, for instance? ▮

A four-footed habitué of the jungle once roamed the streets like an ordinary cat – old Chennai saying. (You'd think any self-respecting national park would have more control over its live-in guests.)

Mr. Carnivore, I presume?

A WHILE AGO, local newspapers heralded the dawn of another brand new, yet typical, Chennai day with the rather alarming announcement that a large and distinctly menacing Big Cat was on the run from the authorities. Homes were immediately in a state of ferment over the possibility of finding one of the bigger and definitely scarier members of the cat family nestling among the potted plants on balconies outside.

The media, in time honoured fashion, helped make life even more interesting by carrying nerve-racking stories of animal sightings in the oddest and most unexpected of places.

Let's get something clear – one has nothing but respect-filled affection for the various species with whom one shares the planet…even if some of them have more claws, teeth, hair, and testier dispositions than is desirable in any acquaintance.

Locating the panther is my "top" priority!

The only cxpcctation, (humble request, actually), is that we all stick to our own territories.

The average citizen has a hard enough time without having to worry about a huge, rather irritated, member of the cat family peering into one's home or car window any moment now.

One understood from the reports that there was much head scratching and many theories over the mysterious marauder, while a local wild life sanctuary tried to ascertain if it was one of their own.

And yet, did the authorities consider this point? If you were a Cat who was part of a cushy zoo system that cared for you, fed you well, and asked nothing more of you than that you occasionally make a frightful face at the humans who came and gazed at you so they could scuttle away thrilled, having got their admission ticket's worth of urban kicks at this close brush with the wild, would you choose to wander off on your own, fending for yourself - even assuming for reasons one cannot even begin to imagine, someone forgot that an enclosed area usually means 4 walls?

I don't think so.

Unless, of course, this was an outsider looking to get in on a good deal.

The media, with its usual penchant for sensitivity, chose to consistently address the Big Cat as the 'carnivore', probably setting its back up no end. After all, maybe it was a gentle soul happiest amongst his sprouts and salads.

The story soon died down, like all such stories. One assumes the Big Cat turned up eventually, rather abashed at having caused all this fuss and bother.

One can only hope that the humans concerned received him with the courtesy he deserved. ▮

You better dress right, be seen at the right places at the right time, nod your head wisely and vehemently signal appreciation with a wave of your hand even if you have no clue what just happened on stage – it takes effort, you know, to be a true Chennai-ite in December.

THE RIGHT NOTE

COME DECEMBER – and Chennai breaks out in song and dance.

The Season is a time of intense creativity, breath-taking performances and earnest sabha-hopping.

But, secretly, for many, December means a lot more than mere Art.

(Note: No offence is intended towards the Arts. The writer doffs a reverent hat at all the immense talent and knowledge displayed by those both on and off the stage. So all those about to get all touchy and porcupine quills-y, relax, okay?)

For some, December is really all about attire. After all, attending at least two, sometimes even three, events in a day…that's a whole lot of sarees and matching jewelry to plan for. The good news is – ethnic chic rubs sophisticated shoulders with good old pattu podavais quite comfortably these days.

For others, flitting between sabhas means they get to check out the new line of young adults on display and go bride-or-groom-hunting as a sort of side benefit to the Season.

You know, Alwarpet Alamelu's recital is accompanied by Natesan's bonda and Saidapet Shankar's by Cheenu's badam kheer… how do we choose between the two?

The harassed souls darting about are, of course, our NRI cousins, who arrive in invasion strength, attempting to pack in both 'catching kutcherys' and hectic family visits in about two weeks. They stand apart, especially the ladies, thanks to their slightly out-moded choli sleeves and kurta lengths. Can't blame them though – fashion changes too quickly for almost everyone.

One of the Season's most distinctive features is the speed with which shared season tickets whiz between sabhas. This relay-race requires patience, competent juggling skills….

and a good memory. Otherwise, rasikas end up in sabha lobbies, staring thoughtfully at the tickets they hold, knowing they were supposed to be handed over to someone somewhere sometime...except they've forgotten who, where, and when.

Then there's the "where's-the-best-food?" competition. This requires a great deal of fine-tuned planning and haring up and down on the part of the rasikas. If breakfast is good in one sabha, lunch at another is to die for. And you haven't lived anyway if you haven't tried the tiffin at yet another venue.

The most glittering luminaries from the world of Dance and Music...combined with good food and camaraderie.

It happens only in Chennai...in December. ▮